MEASURING MANIA

MEASURING TIME WITH A CALENDAR

by Darice Bailer   illustrated by Kathleen Petelinsek

Published in the United States of America by Cherry Lake Publishing
Ann Arbor, Michigan
www.cherrylakepublishing.com

Consultants: Janice Bradley, PhD, Mathematically Connected Communities,
New Mexico State University; Marla Conn, ReadAbility, Inc.

Editorial direction: Red Line Editorial
Book design and illustration: The Design Lab

Photo credits: Hurst Photo/Shutterstock Images, 4; iStockphoto, 5, 14; Mandy
Godbehear/Shutterstock Images, 10; Ingram Publishing/Thinkstock, 12;
Shutterstock Images, 17; Monkey Business Images/Shutterstock Images, 20

Library of Congress Cataloging-in-Publication Data
Bailer, Darice, author.
  Measuring time with a calendar / Darice Bailer.
      pages cm. — (Measuring mania)
  Audience: 5–8.
  Audience: K to grade 3.
  Includes bibliographical references and index.
  ISBN 978-1-62431-649-4 (hardcover) — ISBN 978-1-62431-676-0 (pbk.) —
ISBN 978-1-62431-703-3 (pdf) — ISBN 978-1-62431-730-9 (hosted ebook)
  1. Calendar—Juvenile literature. 2. Planning—Juvenile literature. 3. Time—Juvenile
literature. I. Title.

  CE13.B35 2014
  529'.3—dc23

                                    2013029073

Cherry Lake Publishing would like to acknowledge
the work of The Partnership for 21st Century Skills.
Please visit www.p21.org for more information.

Printed in the United States of America
Corporate Graphics Inc.
January 2014

Table of Contents

CHAPTER ONE
What Is a Calendar?

During what month is your birthday?

How many **days** until your friend's sleepover? How many **weeks** until your birthday party? How many **months** until winter?

We can use a **calendar** to measure time. A calendar keeps track of the days, weeks, and months of the **year**.

Calendars show days, weeks, and months.

A calendar helps you know when school starts. You see when holidays will happen. You can count the weeks until your birthday. Or count the days until your family trip. Let's measure time with a calendar!

To do the activities in this book, you will need:

- 12 index cards or small pieces of paper
- scissors
- marker
- watch with a hand that counts seconds
- 2 dice

Gather what you need.

How Does a Calendar Work?

There are seven days in a week. Can you name them? What is your favorite day of the week?

Add up all the weeks. There are 52 each year.

And there are 12 months for you to count. February is the shortest month. It has 28 or 29 days. The other months have 30 or 31 days.

Sunday

Monday

Tuesday

Wednesday

Thursday

Friday

Saturday

Months of
the Year

| January | February | March | April | May | June |

8

ACTIVITY

What's Missing?

Two months are missing here. Which are they?

January

February

March

April

May

July

August

September

October

November

Use a poem to remember how many days are in each month.

> *Thirty days in September,*
> *April, June, and November.*
> *February has 28 days, but to be clear*
> *It leaps to 29 every four years!*
> *Then there are 7 months with 31 days that fly*
> *March, May, August, and July*
> *And 31 days to also remember*
> *In January, October, and December!*

January is the first month of the year. December is the twelfth and last. Then a whole new year begins on January 1!

We say "Happy New Year" on January 1.

10

The Months of the Year

INSTRUCTIONS:

1. Take 12 index cards. Small pieces of paper work, too. Write the name of one month on each card. Stack them up in a pile.
2. Find or borrow a watch with a second hand. And find a friend.
3. Mix up all the index cards.
4. Work together to put the months in order. Use the watch to time yourselves. Now try to beat your team time!

To get a copy of this activity, visit www.cherrylakepublishing.com/activities.

CHAPTER THREE

A Monthly Plan

Do you play sports or take lessons? How do you keep track of your activities?

Zara and Carter are getting ready for summer. They're making a calendar for July. They want to plan for Zara's swim class. Carter's grandma is coming to visit, too.

Carter drew all the rows and **columns** with a ruler. Then Zara wrote the month and the days of the week at the top.

Zara can make a new calendar every month.

13

Zara and Carter check their calendar. They can see on which day of the week each date falls. They can keep track of their summer fun.

Grandma arrives

Swim lessons

Birthday Party

Fireworks

Write your activities on a calendar to keep track.

ACTIVITY

Can you help Zara and Carter figure a few things out this summer?

INSTRUCTIONS:

1. Carter and Zara are watching the fireworks on July 4. What day of the week is it?
2. Carter's grandma is coming to visit on the Monday after July 4. What date does her visit begin?
3. Carter's grandma is leaving on July 20. What day of the week is that?
4. Zara has a swim meet every Monday in July. How many times will she race with the team this summer?
5. Can Carter's grandma go to any of Zara's swim meets? Which ones can she see?
6. Carter's birthday is five days before his grandma leaves. When is his birthday?

To get a copy of this activity, visit
www.cherrylakepublishing.com/activities.

15

CHAPTER FOUR

From Words to Numbers

February usually has 28 days. But every four years, it has 29 days.

Carter wonders why some years have 365 days but a **leap year** has 366. Zara knows the answer!

It takes Earth one year, or 365 days, five hours, and a little over 48 minutes, to go around the sun. But a calendar year is only 365 days long. So every year on the calendar is a little shorter than an actual year. The fourth year has one day added to make up for that.

Earth and the other planets rotate around the sun. One trip around the sun is one year!

March 31, 2008
3 | 31 / 2008

Write your birthday using words. Then write it using only numbers.

Zara wants to write down her birthday using all numbers. She learned how to do it in school. The teacher wrote the date on the board each day. Zara knows that March is the third month. She writes her birthday two ways: March 31, 2008, and 3/31/2008.

Zara shows Carter how to write his birthday with numbers, too. Carter's birthday is July 15, 2006. Carter writes 7/15/2006. He can shorten it to 7/15/06. Or he can put the year first, 2006/7/15.

Monthly Roll

Take turns rolling a pair of dice with a friend. Then call out the name of the month that goes with that number. For example, if you roll a two, shout, "February!" February is the second month of the year.

   Now play the game a different way. Roll one die. Call out the month. It will be one of the first six months of the year. Then roll the second die. Count forward that many months. For example, suppose you roll a one with the first die. You would call out, "January!" Then you roll a five. What month comes five months after January?

To get a copy of this activity, visit www.cherrylakepublishing.com/activities.

Nine dots are showing. September is the ninth month.

CHAPTER FIVE

You Can Measure Time

Keep track of days, weeks, and months on your own calendar.

You can make your own calendar with paper. You can write the days and weeks. You can keep track of your birthday. Or your family's birthdays. You will know when Grandma is coming to visit and when vacation begins.

Here are more fun ways to measure time with a calendar:

- Look at next year's calendar. On what day of the week is your birthday?

- What is your favorite holiday? On which day of the week will it happen next?

- How many months, weeks, and days are there between your birthday and your favorite holiday?

- Your "golden birthday" is the year your age matches your birth date. If your birthday is September 9, your golden birthday is when you turn nine years old. Have you had your golden birthday? If so, what year was it? If not, in what year will it be?

- In what year will your birthday next fall on a Saturday?

Glossary

calendar (KAL-uhn-dur) a chart to help you keep track of the days, weeks, and months of the year

columns (KAH-luhms) lines of numbers or words going up and down

date (DATE) a specific day

days (DAYS) periods of 24 hours from midnight to midnight

leap year (LEEP YEER) the year every four years when an extra day is added to February for a total of 366 days

months (MUNTHS) the 12 unequal periods that make up the year

weeks (WEEKS) periods of seven days

year (YEER) a measure of time with 12 months and four seasons

For More Information

BOOKS

Gleick, Beth. *Time is When*. Toronto, Ontario: Tundra Books, 2008.

Maestro, Betsy. *The Story of Clocks and Calendars*. New York: HarperCollins Publishers, 2004.

Sweeney, Joan. *Me Counting Time: From Seconds to Centuries*. New York: Dragonfly Books, 2001.

WEB SITES

IXL—Read a Calendar
http://www.ixl.com/math/grade-2/read-a-calendar
How many Fridays are in July? What is the fourth Sunday in August?
There are plenty of questions to help you measure time on a calendar.

Study Jams—Using a Calendar
http://studyjams.scholastic.com/studyjams/jams/math/measurement/using-a-calendar.htm
Test yourself! Check out a calendar to figure out the answers to different questions.

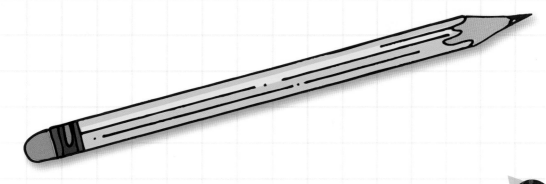

Index

About the Author

Darice Bailer is always checking the calendar to remember when birthdays and holidays are and to tell her when she needs to be at school. She volunteers at Old Greenwich School in Connecticut and is the author of many books for young readers.